One-Minute Pocket Bible for Men

The New King James Version

Wisdom is the principal thing; therefore get
wisdom. And in all your getting, get understanding.
Proverbs 4:7

Tulsa, Oklahoma

4th Printing
Over 60,000 in Print

One-Minute Pocket Bible For Men
ISBN 1-56292-081-2
Copyright © 1994 by Mike Murdock
P.O. Box 99
Dallas, Texas 75221

Published by Honor Books
P.O. Box 55388
Tulsa, OK 74153

This

One-Minute Pocket Bible for Men
The New King James Version

Presented to

Mr. Oldenkamp

By

Nickey & Judy Hodges

Date

2-12-97

Contents

Facts About Men

You were created for a purpose. There is a perfect plan for your life. Never forget God created you for a specific *assignment*.

He loves you.

He planned you.

He scheduled your birth.

He is forever linked to you.

In fact, God loves you so much that He sent His Son, Jesus, to help you. Jesus wants to help you fulfill all the dreams God created you to accomplish on this earth. All you have to do is ask Him. "...Ask and you will receive, that your joy may be full" (John 16:24).

Your purpose is not your decision but your discovery.

When I was a teenager, I heard a story about a farmer whose son went off to college. The father was a bit concerned over the exposure his son would have to atheistic teaching. He knew how articulate and seductive these skilled communicators could be in spreading their own disease of doubt.

His fears were eventually confirmed. His son returned home for a visit, obviously grappling with his faith in God.

As they were conversing one day under an old oak tree, the son suddenly blurted out, "Dad, I just can't believe in God anymore. Why, look at those pumpkins over there on the ground. They are big and heavy, yet have small and tender vines.

"But, this big oak tree, capable of supporting the weight of the pumpkins, only produces tiny acorns. If there was really an intelligent God of this universe. He would have placed the pumpkin on this oak tree, and the tiny acorn on the fragile vine.

Suddenly, an acorn fell from the tree, bouncing lightly off the top of the young man's head.

As the truth slowly dawned, he sheepishly spoke, "Dad, thank God that was not a pumpkin."

Throughout your lifetime, you, too, may question the existence of your Creator. Your logic will always compete with your faith. Your mind will compete with your heart. Just think again.

A book is proof of an *author*.

A poem is proof of a *poet*.

A song is proof of a *composer*.

A product is proof of a *manufacturer*.

Creation is proof of a Creator. Only fools think they arrived first. The fool has said in his heart, "There is no God" (Psalm 14:1a).

The proof of God's presence far outweighs the proof of His absence.

God exists.

The world is arranged...therefore, *an Arranger* must exist.

You see, someday it will hit you like a bolt of lightning — your Creator is a Planner...incredibly organized...meticulous with detail...and, like any successful manufacturer, He is totally committed to the success of His product...YOU.

Why did God create you?

You were created to be an instrument of pleasure to God.

10

You are worthy, O Lord, to receive glory and
honor and power; for You created all things,
and by Your will they exist and were created.

Revelations 4:11

When you pleasure God, He pleasures you.
...if you diligently obey the voice of the Lord
your God, to observe carefully all His commandments which I command you today, that
the Lord your God will set you high above all
nations on the earth.

Deuteronomy 28:1,2

**God is pleasured through daily acts of obedi-
ence that progressively complete His dreams and
goals in your life.**

And whatever we ask we receive from Him,
because we keep His commandments and do
those things that are pleasing in His sight.

1 John 3:22

**Your strongest desires, talents and opportuni-
ties reveal God's calling and dream for your life.**

Having then gifts differing according to the
grace that is given to us, let us use them: if
prophecy...or ministry...he who teaches...he
who exhorts...he who gives...he who leads...he
who shows mercy....

Romans 12:6-8

A Man's Prayer

Dear Heavenly Father,

I know You *do* exist.

I know You created me. I know You created me for a purpose. You have a perfect plan for my life.

Thank You for that plan. Thank You for loving me. I am forever linked to You.

Father, help me to remember that I was created to be an instrument of pleasure to You.

I want to obey You. Put me in remembrance of Your commandments so that I will do those things that are pleasing in Your sight.

Thank You for helping me to discover my talents and my purpose in life. Thank You for being totally committed to my success

In Jesus Name,

Amen.

One-Minute Pocket Bible for Men

The New King James Version

ABILITIES

For the LORD will be your confidence.

Proverbs 3:26a

"Not by might nor by power, but by My Spirit," Says the LORD of hosts.

Zechariah 4:6b

Most assuredly, I say to you, he who believes in Me, the works that I do he will do also; and greater works than these he will do, because I go to My Father.

John 14:12

What then shall we say to these things? If God is for us, who can be against us?

Romans 8:31

But we have the mind of Christ.

1 Corinthians 2:16b

Let him who is taught the word share in all good things with him who teaches.

Galatians 6:9

I can do all things through Christ who strengthens me.

Philippians 4:13

For the gifts and the calling of God are irrevocable.

Romans 11:29

Nothing is ever as difficult as it first appears.

ACHIEVEMENT

LORD, all my desire is before You.

Psalm 38:9a

The soul of a lazy man desires, and has nothing; but the soul of the diligent shall be made rich.

Proverbs 13:4

So shall My word be that goes forth from My mouth; it shall not return to Me void, but it shall accomplish what I please, and it shall prosper in the thing for which I sent it.

Isaiah 55:11

The LORD is good to those who wait for Him, to the soul who seeks Him.

Lamentations 3:25

Therefore I say to you, whatever things you ask when you pray, believe that you receive them, and you will have them.

Mark 11:24

But without faith it is impossible to please Him, for he who comes to God must believe that He is, and that He is a rewarder of those who diligently seek Him.

Hebrews 11:6

Every creation contains an invisible command from God to multiply and become more.

ANGER

So then, my beloved brethren, let every man be swift to hear, slow to speak, slow to wrath; for the wrath of man does not produce the righteousness of God.

James 1:19,20

"Be angry, and do not sin": do not let the sun go down on your wrath.

Ephesians 4:26

A soft answer turns away wrath, but a harsh word stirs up anger.

Proverb 15:1

Beloved, do not avenge yourselves, but rather give place to wrath; for it is written, "Vengeance Is Mine, I will repay," says the Lord.

Romans 12:19

Do not hasten in your spirit to be angry, for anger rests in the bosom of fools

Ecclesiastes 7:9

Your entry can decide how you exit.

APPEARANCE

But the LORD said to Samuel, "Do not look at his appearance or at the height of his stature, because I have refused him. For the Lord does not see as man sees; for man looks at the outward appearance, but the LORD looks at the heart."

1 Samuel 16:7

For the LORD takes pleasure in His people; He will beautify the humble with salvation.

Psalm 149:4

A merry heart makes a cheerful countenance, but by sorrow of the heart the spirit is broken.

Proverbs 15:13

Do you look at things according to the outward appearance? If anyone is convinced in himself that he is Christ's, let him again consider this in himself, that just as he is Christ's, even so we are Christ's.

2 Corinthians 10:7

Do not let your adornment be merely outward; arranging the hair, wearing gold, or putting on fine apparel; rather let it be the hidden person of the heart, with the incorruptible beauty of a gentle and quiet spirit, which is very precious in the sight of God.

1 Peter 3:3,4

People see what you are before they hear what you are.

ASSIGNMENT

Let each one remain in the same calling in which he was called.

1 Corinthians 7:20

And let the beauty of the LORD our God be upon us, and establish the work of our hands for us; yes, establish the work of our hands.

Psalm 90:17

Your ears shall hear a word behind you, saying, "This is the way, walk in it." Whenever you turn to the right hand or whenever you turn to the left.

Isaiah 30:21

Do you see a man who excels in his work? He will stand before kings; he will not stand before unknown men.

Proverbs 22:29

For exaltation comes neither from the east nor from the west nor from the south. But God is the Judge: He puts down one, and exalts another.

Psalm 75:6,7

Your assignment is decided by God and discovered by you. It is geographical and is always to a person or people. It is always to solve a problem for someone.

ATTITUDE

Teach me, and I will hold my tongue; cause me to understand wherein I have erred.

Job 6:24

For out of the abundance of the heart the mouth speaks. But I say to you that for every idle word men may speak, they will give account of it in the day of judgment. For by your words you will be justified, and by your words you will be condemned.

Matthew 12:34b,36,37

"Be angry, and do not sin": do not let the sun go down on your wrath.

Ephesians 4:26

Do not grumble against one another, brethren, lest you be condemned. Behold, the Judge is standing at the door!

James 5:9

Let your conduct be without covetousness; be content with such things as you have. For He Himself has said, "I will never leave you nor forsake you."

Hebrews 13:5

**Your attitude determines
the seasons you enter.**

BIBLE

You shall not add to the word which I command you, nor take from it, that you may keep the commandments of the LORD your God which I command you.

Deuteronomy 4:2

The law of the LORD is perfect, converting the soul; the testimony of the LORD is sure, making wise the simple.

Psalm 19:7

Your word I have hidden in my heart, that I might not sin against You! Your word is a lamp to my feet and a light to my path.

Psalm 119:11,105

Heaven and earth will pass away, but My words will by no means pass away.

Mark 13:31

All Scripture is given by Inspiration of God, and is profitable for doctrine, for reproof, for correction, for instruction in righteousness, that the man of God may be complete, thoroughly equipped for every good work.

2 Timothy 3:16,17

For the word of God is living and powerful, and sharper than any two-edged sword, piercing even to the division of soul and spirit, and of joints and marrow, and is a discerner of the thoughts and intents of the heart.

Hebrews 4:12

**God's only need is to be believed.
His only pain is to be doubted.**

CHILDREN

The righteous man walks in his integrity; his children are blessed after him.

Proverbs 20:7

Behold, children are a heritage from the LORD, the fruit of the womb is a reward.

Psalm 127:3

Whoever receives one little child like this in My name receives Me.

Matthew 18:5

Train up a child in the way he should go, and when he is old he will not depart from it.

Proverbs 22:6

Only you know your priorities.

CHURCH ATTENDANCE

And let them make Me a sanctuary, that I may dwell among them.

Exodus 25:8

One thing I have desired of the LORD, that will I seek: that I may dwell in the house of the LORD all the days of my life, to behold the beauty of the LORD, and to inquire in His temple.

Psalm 27:4

I was glad when they said to me, "Let us go into the house of the LORD."

Psalm 122:1

Walk prudently when you go to the house of God; and draw near to hear rather than to give the sacrifice of fools, for they do not know that they do evil.

Ecclesiastes 5:1

For where two or three are gathered together in My name, I am there in the midst of them.

Matthew 18:20

Not forsaking the assembling of ourselves together, as is the manner of some, but exhorting one another, and so much the more as you see the Day approaching.

Hebrews 10:25

Climate determines what grows within you.

COMMITMENT

Commit your way to the LORD, trust also in Him, and He shall bring it to pass.

Psalm 37:5

Commit your works to the LORD, and your thoughts will be established.

Proverbs 16:3

He did not waver at the promise of God through unbelief, but was strengthened in faith, giving glory to God, and being fully convinced that what He had promised He was also able to perform.

Romans 4:20,21

And let us not grow weary while doing good, for in due season we shall reap if we do not lose heart.

Galatians 6:9

Brethren, I do not count myself to have apprehended; but one thing I do, forgetting those things which are behind and reaching forward to those things which are ahead, I press toward the goal for the prize of the upward call of God in Christ Jesus.

Philippians 3:13,14

Commitment is your final decision to meet the needs of the ones God has called you to serve.

COMMUNICATION

Your ears shall hear a word behind you, saying, "This is the way, walk in it," whenever you turn to the right hand or whenever you turn to the left.

Isaiah 30:21

Do not be deceived: "Evil company corrupts good habits."

1 Corinthians 15:33

Let him who is taught the word share in all good things with him who teaches.

Galatians 6:6

Let no corrupt word proceed out of your mouth, but what is good for necessary edification, that it may impart grace to the hearers.

Ephesians 4:29

Nevertheless you have done well that you shared in my distress.

Philippians 4:14

But now you yourselves are to put off all these: anger, wrath, malice, blasphemy, filthy language out of your mouth.

Colossians 3:8

If what you say to someone cannot be said to everyone, then say it to no one!
J. E. Murdock

COMPASSION

But He, being full of compassion, forgave their iniquity, and did not destroy them. Yes, many a time He turned His anger away, and did not stir up all His wrath.

Psalm 78:38

Unto the upright there arises light in the darkness; he is gracious, and full of compassion, and righteous.

Psalm 112:4

Can a woman forget her nursing child, and not have compassion on the son of her womb? Surely they may forget, yet I will not forget you.

Isaiah 49:15

And Jesus, when He came out, saw a great multitude and was moved with compassion for them, because they were like sheep not having a shepherd. So He began to teach them many things.

Mark 6:34

Finally, all of you be of one mind, having compassion for one another; love as brothers, be tenderhearted, be courteous.

1 Peter 3:8

Those who unlock your compassion are those to whom you have been assigned.

COURAGE

Be strong and of good courage, do not fear nor be afraid of them; for the LORD your God, He is the One who goes with you. He will not leave you nor forsake you.

Deuteronomy 31:6

Have I not commanded you? Be strong and of good courage; do not be afraid, nor be dismayed, for the LORD your God is with you wherever you go.

Joshua 1:9

Be of good courage, and He shall strengthen your heart, all you who hope in the LORD.

Psalm 31:24

No evil shall befall you, nor shall any plague come near your dwelling.

Psalm 91:10

Fear not, for I am with you; be not dismayed, for I am your God. I will strengthen you, yes, I will help you, I will uphold you with My righteous right hand.

Isaiah 41:10

I can do all things through Christ who strengthens me.

Philippians 4:13

Winners are just ex-losers who got mad.

CRISIS

Yea, though I walk through the valley of the shadow of death, I will fear no evil; for You are with me; Your rod and Your staff, they comfort me.

Psalm 23:4

For in the time of trouble He shall hide me in His pavilion; in the secret place of His tabernacle He shall hide me; He shall set me high upon a rock.

Psalm 27:5

My soul shall make its boast in the LORD; the humble shall hear of it and be glad. Oh, magnify the LORD with me, and let us exalt His name together. I sought the LORD, and He heard me, and delivered me from all my fears.

Psalm 34:2-4

God is our refuge and strength, a very present help in trouble. Therefore we will not fear, even though the earth be removed, and though the mountains be carried into the midst of the sea; though its waters roar and be troubled, though the mountains shake with its swelling. Selah

Psalm 46:1-3

I will not leave you orphans; I will come to you.

John 14:18

Crisis always occurs at the curve of change.

CRITICISM

A soft answer turns away wrath, but a harsh word stirs up anger.

Proverbs 15:1

Blessed are you when they revile and persecute you, and say all kinds of evil against you falsely for My sake.

Matthew 5:11

But I say to you, love your enemies, bless those who curse you, do good to those who hate you, and pray for those who spitefully use you and persecute you.

Matthew 5:44

Likewise the soldiers asked him, saying, "And what shall we do?" So he said to them, "Do not intimidate anyone or accuse falsely, and be content with your wages."

Luke 3:14

But love your enemies, do good, and lend, hoping for nothing in return; and your reward will be great, and you will be sons of the Most High. For He is kind to the unthankful and evil.

Luke 6:35

Having a good conscience, that when they defame you as evildoers, those who revile your good conduct in Christ may be ashamed.

1 Peter 3:16

Never spend more time on a critic than you would give to a friend.

DEBT

The wicked borrows and does not repay, but the right-eous shows mercy and gives.

Psalm 37:21

He who is surety for a stranger will suffer, but one who hates being surety is secure.

Proverbs 11:15

The rich rules over the poor, and the borrower is servant to the lender.

Proverbs 22:7

Give, and it will be given to you: good measure, pressed down, shaken together, and running over will be put into your bosom. For with the same measure that you use, it will.be measured back to you.

Luke 6:38

Owe no one anything except to love one another.

Romans 13:8a

Beloved, I pray that you may prosper in all things and be in health, just as your soul prospers.

3 John 2

You shall lend to many nations, but you shall not borrow.
Deuteronomy 28:12b

Debt is proof of greed. It is the opposite of giving. Debt is emptying your future to fill up your present. Giving is emptying your present to fill up your future.

DECISION MAKING

And if it seems evil to you to serve the LORD, choose for yourselves this day whom you will serve, whether the gods which your fathers served that were on the other side of the River, or the gods of the Amorites, in whose land you dwell. But as for me and my house, we will serve the LORD.

Joshua 24:15

Trust in the LORD with all your heart, and lean not on your own understanding; in all your ways acknowledge Him, and He shall direct your paths.

Proverbs 3:5,6

He who heeds the word wisely will find good, and whoever trusts in the LORD, happy is he.

Proverbs 16:20

But Daniel purposed in his heart that he would not defile himself with the portion of the king's delicacies, nor with the wine which he drank; therefore he requested of the chief of the eunuchs that he might not defile himself.

Daniel 1:8

So let each one give as he purposes in his heart, not grudgingly or of necessity; for God loves a cheerful giver.

2 Corinthians 9:7

Champions make decisions that create the future they desire while losers make decisions that create the present they desire.

DEPRESSION

But You, O LORD, are a shield for me, my glory and the One who lifts up my head. I cried to the LORD with my voice, and He heard me from His holy hill. I lay down and slept; I awoke, for the LORD sustained me.

Psalm 3:3-5

Weeping may endure for a night, but joy comes in the morning.

Psalm 30:5b

Our soul waits for the LORD; He is our help and our shield.

Psalm 33:20

Why are you cast down, O my soul? And why are you disquieted within me? Hope in God; for I shall yet praise Him, the help of my countenance and my God.

Psalm 42:11

The LORD shall preserve your going out and your coming in from this time forth, and even forevermore.

Psalm 121:8

He heals the brokenhearted and binds up their wounds.

Psalm 147:3

Struggle is the proof you have not yet been conquered. Warfare always surrounds the birth of a miracle.

DESIRE

Delight yourself also in the LORD, and He shall give you the desires of your heart.

Psalm 37:4

Lord, all my desire is before You; and my sighing is not hidden from You.

Psalm 38:9

And there is none upon earth that I desire besides You.

Psalm 73:25b

A desire accomplished is sweet to the soul.

Proverbs 13:19a

And whatever things you ask in prayer, believing, you will receive.

Matthew 21:22

Therefore I say to you, whatever things you ask when you pray, believe that you receive them, and you will have them.

Mark 11:24

So I say to you, ask, and it will be given to you; seek, and you will find; knock, and it will be opened to you.

Luke 11:9

The proof of desire is pursuit. You will never possess what you are unwilling to pursue. Desire is not what you want it's what you cannot live without.

DILIGENCE

He who has a slack hand becomes poor, but the hand of the diligent makes rich. He who gathers in summer is a wise son; he who sleeps in harvest is a son who causes shame.

Proverbs 10:4,5

The hand of the diligent will rule. But diligence is man's precious possession.

Proverbs 12:24a,27b

The soul of a lazy man desires, and has nothing; but the soul of the diligent shall be made rich.

Proverbs 13:4

Do you see a man who excels in his work? He will stand before kings; he will not stand before unknown men.

Proverbs 22:29

Whatever your hand finds to do, do it with your might.

Ecclesiastes 9:10a

I can do all things through Christ who strengthens me.

Philippians 4:13

Diligence is speedy attention to an assigned task. It is insistence upon completion.

DISAPPOINTMENT

Have I not commanded you? Be strong and of good courage; do not be afraid, nor be dismayed, for the LORD your God is with you wherever you go.

Joshua 1:9

The LORD is my light and my salvation; whom shall I fear? The LORD is the strength of my life; of whom shall I be afraid? When the wicked came against me to eat up my flesh, my enemies and foes, they stumbled and fell. Though an army may encamp against me, my heart shall not fear; though war should rise against me, in this I will be confident.

Psalm 27:1-3

I will lift up my eyes to the hills; from whence comes my help? My help comes from the LORD, who made heaven and earth.

Psalm 121:1,2

And we know that all things work together for good to those who love God, to those who are called according to His purpose. What then shall we say to these things? If God is for us, who can be against us?

Romans 8:28,31

**Tomorrow contains more joy than
any yesterday you can recall.**

DISCIPLINE

Teach me to do Your will, for You are my God; Your Spirit is good. Lead me in the land of uprightness.

Psalm 143:10

He who spares his rod hates his son, but he who loves him disciplines him promptly.

Proverbs 13:24

Chasten your son while there is hope, and do not set your heart on his destruction.

Proverbs 19:18

Train up a child in the way he should go, and when he is old he will not depart from it. Foolishness is bound up in the heart of a child; the rod of correction will drive it far from him.

Proverbs 22:6,15

O LORD, correct me, but with justice; not in Your anger, lest You bring me to nothing.

Jeremiah 10:24

For whom the LORD loves He chastens, and scourges every son whom He receives. If you endure chastening, God deals with you as with sons; for what son is there whom a father does not chasten? But if you are without chastening, of which all have become partakers, then you are illegitimate and not sons.

Hebrews 12:6-8

Champions are willing to do things they hate, to create something they love.

40

DISCRETION

Therefore give to Your servant an understanding heart to judge Your people, that I may discern between good and evil. For who is able to judge this great people of Yours?

1 Kings 3:9

Blessed is the man who walks not in the counsel of the ungodly, nor stands in the path of sinners, nor sits in the seat of the scornful; but his delight is in the law of the LORD, and in His law he meditates day and night. He shall be like a tree planted by the rivers of water, that brings forth its fruit in its season, whose leaf also shall not wither; and whatever he does shall prosper.

Psalm 1:1-3

A good man deals graciously and lends; he will guide his affairs with discretion.

Psalm 112:5

I am Your servant; give me understanding, that I may know Your testimonies. The entrance of Your words gives light; it gives understanding to the simple.

Psalm 119:125,130

Trust in the LORD with all your heart, and lean not on your own understanding; in all your ways acknowledge Him, and He shall direct your paths.

Proverbs 3:5,6

Never discuss your problem with someone who cannot solve it. Silence cannot be misquoted.

ENTHUSIASM

Let the heavens rejoice, and let the earth be glad; and let them say among the nations, "The LORD reigns."

1 Chronicles 16:31

You have turned for me my mourning into dancing.

Psalm 30:11a

Oh, clap your hands, all you peoples! Shout to God with the voice of triumph!

Psalm 47:1

Blessed are the people who know the joyful sound! They walk, O LORD, in the light of Your countenance.

Psalm 89:15

A merry heart makes a cheerful countenance.

Proverbs 15:13a

For you shall go out with joy, and be led out with peace.

Isaiah 55:12a

Speaking to one another in psalms and hymns and spiritual songs, singing and making melody in your heart to the Lord.

Ephesians 5:19

The atmosphere you permit determines the product you produce.

ETHICS

You shall not bear false witness against your neighbor.

Exodus 20:16

Blessed is the man who walks not in the counsel of the ungodly, nor stands in the path of sinners, nor sits in the seat of the scornful; but his delight is in the law of the LORD, and in His law he meditates day and night.

Psalm 1:1,2

Let integrity and uprightness preserve me, for I wait for You.

Psalm 25:21

Vindicate me, O LORD, for I have walked in my integrity. I have also trusted in the LORD; I shall not slip.

Psalm 26:1

The righteous man walks in his integrity; his children are blessed after him.

Proverbs 20:7

Repay no one evil for evil. Have regard for good things in the sight of all men.

Romans 12:17

What you are is revealed by what you do.
What you do reveals what you really believe.

EXCELLENCE

Yet the righteous will hold to his way, and he who has clean hands will be stronger and stronger.

Job 17:9

The righteous shall flourish like a palm tree, he shall grow like a cedar in Lebanon.

Psalm 92:12

A good name is to be chosen rather than great riches, loving favor rather than silver and gold.

Proverbs 22:1

So the governors and satraps sought to find some charge against Daniel concerning the kingdom; but they could find no charge or fault, because he was faithful; nor was there any error or fault found in him.

Daniel 6:4

But as you abound in everything; in faith, in speech, in knowledge, in all diligence, and in your love for us; see that you abound in this grace also.

2 Corinthians 8:7

You will only have significant success with something that is an obsession.

EXPECTATION

Why are you cast down, O my soul? And why are you disquieted within me? Hope in God; for I shall yet praise Him, the help of my countenance and my God.

Psalm 42:11

My soul, wait silently for God alone, for my expectation is from Him.

Psalm 62:5

For surely there is a hereafter, and your hope will not be cut off.

Proverbs 23:18

Jesus said to him, "If you can believe, all things are possible to him who believes."

Mark 9:23

"For assuredly, I say to you, whoever says to this mountain, 'Be removed and be cast into the sea,' and does not doubt in his heart, but believes that those things he says will be done, he will have whatever he says. Therefore I say to you, whatever things you ask when you pray, believe that you receive them, and you will have them."

Mark 11:23,24

But without faith it is impossible to please Him, for he who comes to God must believe that He is, and that He is a rewarder of those who diligently seek Him.

Hebrews 11:6

The seasons of your life will change every time you decide to use your faith.

FAITH

And whatever things you ask in prayer, believing, you will receive.

Matthew 21:22

Jesus said to him, "If you can believe, all things are possible to him who believes."

Mark 9:23

So the Lord said, "If you have faith as a mustard seed, you can say to this mulberry tree, 'Be pulled up by the roots and be planted in the sea,' and it would obey you."

Luke 17:6

Therefore I say to you, whatever things you ask when you pray, believe that you receive them, and you will have them.

Mark 11:24

He did not waver at the promise of God through unbelief, but was strengthened in faith, giving glory to God, and being fully convinced that what He had promised He was also able to perform.

Romans 4:20,21

Above all, taking the shield of faith with which you will be able to quench all the fiery darts of the wicked one.

Ephesians 6:16

When you want something you've never had you've got to do something you've never done.

FAMILY

Train up a child in the way he should go, and when he is old he will not depart from it.

Proverbs 22:6

The father of the righteous will greatly rejoice, and he who begets a wise child will delight in him.

Proverbs 23:24

Through wisdom a house is built, and by understanding it is established.

Proverbs 24:3

All your children shall be taught by the LORD, and great shall be the peace of your children.

Isaiah 54:13

So they said, "Believe on the Lord Jesus Christ, and you will be saved, you and your household."

Acts 16:31

And you, fathers, do not provoke your children to wrath, but bring them up in the training and admonition of the Lord.

Ephesians 6:4

But if anyone does not provide for his own, and especially for those of his household, he has denied the faith and is worse than an unbeliever.

1 Timothy 5:8

**You are the seed that decides
the harvest around you.**

FAVOR

A good man deals graciously and lends; he will guide his affairs with discretion.

Psalm 112:5

He who earnestly seeks good finds favor, but trouble will come to him who seeks evil.

Proverbs 11:27

A good man obtains favor from the LORD, but a man of wicked intentions He will condemn.

Proverbs 12:2

Good understanding gains favor, but the way of the unfaithful is hard. Every prudent man acts with knowledge, but a fool lays open his folly.

Proverbs 13:15,16

Charm is deceitful and beauty is passing, but a woman who fears the LORD, she shall be praised.

Proverbs 31:30

And Jesus increased in wisdom and stature, and in favor with God and men.

Luke 2:52

Currents of favor begin to flow the moment you solve a problem for someone.

FEAR

Be strong and of good courage, do not fear nor be afraid of them; for the LORD your God, He is the One who goes with you. He will not leave you nor forsake you.

Deuteronomy 31:6

Behold, God is my salvation, I will trust and not be afraid; 'For YAH, the LORD, is my strength and song; He also has become my salvation.'

Isaiah 12:2

Fear not, for I am with you; be not dismayed, for I am your God. I will strengthen you, yes, I will help you, I will uphold you with My righteous right hand.

Isaiah 41:10

For you did not receive the spirit of bondage again to fear, but you received the Spirit of adoption by whom we cry out, "Abba, Father."

Romans 8:15

For God has not given us a spirit of fear, but of power and of love and of a sound mind.

2 Timothy 1:7

**Examine well what you're running from.
You are not prey. Your future is whimpering
at your feet begging for instructions.**

FOCUS

My heart is steadfast, O God, my heart is steadfast; I will sing and give praise.

Psalm 57:7

I press toward the goal for the prize of the upward call of God in Christ Jesus.

Philippians 3:14

Only be strong and very courageous, that you may observe to do according to all the law which Moses My servant commanded you; do not turn from it to the right hand or to the left, that you may prosper wherever you go.

Joshua 1:7

But Jesus said to him, "No one, having put his hand to the plow, and looking back, is fit for the kingdom of God."

Luke 9:62

But from there you will seek the LORD your God, and you will find Him if you seek Him with all your heart and with all your soul.

Deuteronomy 4:29

Therefore you shall be careful to do as the LORD your God has commanded you; you shall not turn aside to the right hand or to the left.

Deuteronomy 5:32

The only reason men fail is broken focus.

FORGIVENESS

The discretion of a man makes him slow to anger, and his glory is to overlook a transgression.

Proverbs 19:11

If your enemy is hungry, give him bread to eat; and if he is thirsty, give him water to drink.

Proverbs 25:21

Blessed are the merciful, for they shall obtain mercy.

Matthew 5:7

But I tell you not to resist an evil person. But whoever slaps you on your right cheek, turn the other to him also.

Matthew 5:39

But if you do not forgive men their trespasses, neither will your Father forgive your trespasses.

Matthew 6:15

And be kind to one another, tenderhearted, forgiving one another, just as God in Christ forgave you.

Ephesians 4:32

Bearing with one another, and forgiving one another.

Colossians 3:13a

Mercy is like money. Your deposits determine your withdrawals.

FRIENDSHIP

Behold, how good and how pleasant it is for brethren to dwell together in unity!

Psalm 133:1

A friend loves at all times, and a brother is born for adversity.

Proverbs 17:17

A man who has friends must himself be friendly, but there is a friend who sticks closer than a brother.

Proverbs 18:24

Make no friendship with an angry man.

Proverbs 22:24a

Faithful are the wounds of a friend, but the kisses of an enemy are deceitful. Ointment and perfume delight the heart, and the sweetness of a man's friend gives delight by hearty counsel. Do not forsake your own friend or your father's friend, nor go to your brother's house in the day of your calamity; better is a neighbor nearby than a brother far away.

Proverbs 27:6,9,10

Greater love has no one than this, than to lay down one's life for his friends. You are My friends if you do whatever I command you.

John 15:13,14

**When God wants to bless you,
He puts a person in your life.**

GOAL SETTING

In all your ways acknowledge Him, and He shall direct your paths.

Proverbs 3:6

The preparations of the heart belong to man, but the answer of the tongue is from the LORD. A man's heart plans his way, but the LORD directs his steps.

Proverbs 16:1,9

For which of you, intending to build a tower, does not sit down first and count the cost, whether he has enough to finish it; lest, after he has laid the foundation, and is not able to finish, all who see it begin to mock him, saying, 'This man began to build and was not able to finish.' Or what king, going to make war against another king, does not sit down first and consider whether he is able with ten thousand to meet him who comes against him with twenty thousand? Or else, while the other is still a great way off, he sends a delegation and asks conditions of peace.

Luke 14:28-32

Go to the ant, you sluggard! Consider her ways and be wise, which, having no captain, overseer or ruler, provides her supplies in the summer, and gathers her food in the harvest.

Proverbs 6:6-8

You will never leave where you are until you decide where you would rather be.

GOD

In the beginning God created the heavens and the earth.

Genesis 1:1

In the beginning was the Word, and the Word was with God, and the Word was God. He was in the beginning with God.

John 1:1,2

For it is written: "As I live, says the LORD, every knee shall bow to Me, and every tongue shall confess to God." So then each of us shall give account of himself to God.

Romans 14:11,12

For by Him all things were created that are in heaven and that are on earth, visible and invisible, whether thrones or dominions or principalities or powers. All things were created through Him and for Him. And He is before all things, and in Him all things consist.

Colossians 1:16,17

Then a voice came from the throne, saying, "Praise our God, all you His servants and those who fear Him, both small and great!"

Revelation 19:5

The fool has said in his heart, "There is no God." They are corrupt, and have done abominable iniquity; there is none who does good.

Psalm 53:1

The evidence of God's presence far outweighs the proof of his absence.

GOSSIP

Whoever secretly slanders his neighbor, him I will destroy; the one who has a haughty look and a proud heart, him I will not endure.

Psalm 101:5

Set a guard, O LORD, over my mouth; keep watch over the door of my lips.

Psalm 141:3

For by your words you will be justified, and by your words you will be condemned.

Matthew 12:37

Let no corrupt word proceed out of your mouth, but what is good for necessary edification, that it may impart grace to the hearers.

Ephesians 4:29

And besides they learn to be idle, wandering about from house to house, and not only idle but also gossips and busybodies, saying things which they ought not.

1 Timothy 5:13

But let none of you suffer as a murderer, a thief, an evil-doer, or as a busybody in other people's matters.

1 Peter 4:15

So then, my beloved brethren, let every man be swift to hear, slow to speak, slow to wrath.

James 1:19

**False accusation is the last stage
before supernatural promotion.**

GRATITUDE

Enter into His gates with thanksgiving, and into His courts with praise. Be thankful to Him, and bless His name.

Psalm 100:4

Then He took the cup, and gave thanks, and said, "Take this and divide it among yourselves." And He took bread, gave thanks and broke it, and gave it to them, saying, "This is My body which is given for you; do this in remembrance of Me."

Luke 22:17,19

Blessed be the God and Father of our Lord Jesus Christ, who has blessed us with every spiritual blessing in the heavenly places in Christ.

Ephesians 1:3

Giving thanks always for all things to God the Father in the name of our Lord Jesus Christ.

Ephesians 5:20

Be anxious for nothing, but in everything by prayer and supplication, with thanksgiving, let your requests be made known to God.

Philippians 4:6

Blessing and glory and wisdom, thanksgiving and honor and power and might, be to our God forever and ever. Amen.

Revelation 7:12b

Gratitude is simply awareness of the givers in your life. You can not name one thing that was not given to you.

GREED

There is one who scatters, yet increases more; and there is one who withholds more than is right, but it leads to poverty. The generous soul will be made rich, and he who waters will also be watered himself.

Proverbs 11:24,25

He who despises his neighbor sins; but he who has mercy on the poor, happy is he.

Proverbs 14:21

He who is greedy for gain troubles his own house.

Proverbs 15:27a

And He said to them, "Take heed and beware of covetousness, for one's life does not consist in the abundance of the things he possesses. For where your treasure is, there your heart will be also."

Luke 12:15,34

For He Himself has said, "I will never leave you nor forsake you."

Hebrews 13:5b

Do not overwork to be rich; because of your own understanding, cease! Will you set your eyes on that which is not? For riches certainly make themselves wings; they fly away like an eagle toward heaven.

Proverbs 23:4,5

**Giving is the only proof that
you have overcome greed.**

GRIEF

But I do not want you to be ignorant, brethren, concerning those who have fallen asleep, lest you sorrow as others who have no hope. For if we believe that Jesus died and rose again, even so God will bring with Him those who sleep in Jesus.

1 Thessalonians 4:13,14

For the LORD has comforted His people, and will have mercy on His afflicted.

Isaiah 49:13b

When you pass through the waters, I will be with you; and through the rivers, they shall not overflow you. When you walk through the fire, you shall not be burned, nor shall the flame scorch you.

Isaiah 43:2

Blessed are those who mourn, for they shall be comforted.

Matthew 5:4

This is my comfort in my affliction, for Your word has given me life.

Psalm 119:50

Adversity is breeding ground for miracles.

GUIDANCE

Your word is a lamp to my feet and a light to my path.

Psalm 119:105

When you roam, they will lead you; when you sleep, they will keep you; and when you awake, they will speak with you. For the commandment is a lamp, and the law a light; reproofs of instruction are the way of life.

Proverbs 6:22,23

Then Jesus said to those Jews who believed Him, "If you abide in My word, you are My disciples indeed. And you shall know the truth, and the truth shall make you free."

John 8:31,32

I will instruct you and teach you in the way you should go; I will guide you with My eye.

Psalm 32:8

All Scripture is given by inspiration of God, and is profitable for doctrine, for reproof, for correction, for instruction in righteousness, that the man of God may be complete, thoroughly equipped for every good work.

2 Timothy 3:16,17

Cultivate a teachable spirit.

HABITS

So I will sing praise to Your name forever, that I may daily perform my vows.

Psalm 61:8

My son, keep my words, and treasure my commands within you.

Proverbs 7:1

Do you not know that to whom you present yourselves slaves to obey, you are that one's slaves whom you obey, whether of sin leading to death, or of obedience leading to righteousness?

Romans 6:16

I say then: Walk in the Spirit, and you shall not fulfill the lust of the flesh.

Galatians 5:16

I can do all things through Christ who strengthens me.

Philippians 4:13

However, for this reason I obtained mercy, that in me first Jesus Christ might show all longsuffering, as a pattern to those who are going to believe on Him for everlasting life.

1 Timothy 1:16

In all things showing yourself to be a pattern of good works; in doctrine showing integrity, reverence, incorruptibility.

Titus 2:7

Men do not decide their future. They decide their habits and their habits decide their future.

HAPPINESS

Behold, happy is the man whom God corrects; therefore do not despise the chastening of the Almighty.

Job 5:17

You have put gladness in my heart, more than in the season that their grain and wine increased.

Psalm 4:7

Happy are the people who are in such a state; happy are the people whose God is the LORD!

Psalm 144:15

He who despises his neighbor sins; but he who has mercy on the poor, happy is he.

Proverbs 14:21

He who heeds the word wisely will find good, and whoever trusts in the LORD, happy is he.

Proverbs 16:20

Where there is no revelation, the people cast off restraint; but happy is he who keeps the law.

Proverbs 29:18

Happy is the man who finds wisdom, and the man who gains understanding.

Proverbs 3:13

**Happy is the man that findeth wisdom.
That is how you know who has it.**

61

HEALTH

He heals the brokenhearted and binds up their wounds.

Psalm 147:3

Do not be wise in your own eyes; fear the LORD and depart from evil. It will be health to your flesh, and strength to your bones.

Proverbs 3:7,8

My son, give attention to my words; incline your ear to my sayings. Do not let them depart from your eyes; keep them in the midst of your heart; for they are life to those who find them, and health to all their flesh.

Proverbs 4:20-22

Pleasant words are like a honeycomb, sweetness to the soul and health to the bones.

Proverbs 16:24

A merry heart does good, like medicine, but a broken spirit dries the bones.

Proverbs 17:22

Beloved, I pray that you may prosper in all things and be in health, just as your soul prospers.

3 John 2

For I am the LORD who heals you.

Exodus 15:26b

For I will restore health to you and heal you of your wounds, says the LORD.

Jeremiah 30:17a

Longevity is the product of wisdom.

HOPE

Therefore my heart is glad, and my glory rejoices; my flesh also will rest in hope.

Psalm 16:9

Be of good courage, and He shall strengthen your heart, all you who hope in the LORD.

Psalm 31:24

Now hope does not disappoint, because the love of God has been poured out in our hearts by the Holy Spirit who was given to us.

Romans 5:5

But if we hope for what we do not see, we eagerly wait for it with perseverance.

Romans 8:25

Now may the God of hope fill you with all joy and peace in believing, that you may abound in hope by the power of the Holy Spirit.

Romans 15:13

**Everything God created is
a solution to a problem.**

HUMILITY

By humility and the fear of the LORD are riches and honor and life.

Proverbs 22:4

Therefore whoever humbles himself as this little child is the greatest in the kingdom of heaven.

Matthew 18:4

Therefore, as the elect of God, holy and beloved, put on tender mercies, kindness, humility, meekness, longsuffering.

Colossians 3:12

And being found in appearance as a man, He humbled Himself and became obedient to the point of death, even the death of the cross.

Philippians 2:8

Therefore humble yourselves under the mighty hand of God, that He may exalt you in due time.

1 Peter 5:6

But He gives more grace. Therefore He says: "God resists the proud, but gives grace to the humble." Humble yourselves in the sight of the Lord, and He will lift you up.

James 4:6,10

**Those in high places can be brought down.
Those in low places can be called up.
Humility is the awareness of it.**

IGNORANCE

The fear of the LORD is the beginning of wisdom; a good understanding have all those who do His commandments. His praise endures forever.

Psalm 111:10

For the LORD gives wisdom; from His mouth come knowledge and understanding; He stores up sound wisdom for the upright; He is a shield to those who walk uprightly.

Proverbs 2:6,7

For this reason we also, since the day we heard it, do not cease to pray for you, and to ask that you may be filled with the knowledge of His will in all wisdom and spiritual understanding; that you may walk worthy of the Lord, fully pleasing Him, being fruitful in every good work and increasing in the knowledge of God.

Colossians 1:9,10

My people are destroyed for lack of knowledge. Because you have rejected knowledge, I also will reject you from being priest for Me; because you have forgotten the law of your God, I also will forget your children.

Hosea 4:6

You will never change what you

believe until your belief system cannot produce something you want.

INFORMATION

The entrance of Your words gives light; it gives understanding to the simple.

Psalm 119:130

Whoever loves instruction loves knowledge, but he who hates correction is stupid.

Proverbs 12:1

For God gives wisdom and knowledge and joy to a man who is good in His sight.

Ecclesiastes 2:26a

My people are destroyed for lack of knowledge. Because you have rejected knowledge, I also will reject you from being priest for Me; because you have forgotten the law of your God, I also will forget your children.

Hosea 4:6

For this reason we also, since the day we heard it, do not cease to pray for you, and to ask that you may be filled with the knowledge of His will in all wisdom and spiritual understanding; that you may walk worthy of the Lord, fully pleasing Him, being fruitful in every good work and increasing in the knowledge of God.

Colossians 1:9,10

The difference in people is between their ears. The difference between your present and your future is information.

INTEGRITY

Let me be weighed on honest scales, that God may know my integrity.

Job 31:6

Blessed is the man who walks not in the counsel of the ungodly, nor stands in the path of sinners, nor sits in the seat of the scornful.

Psalm 1:1

The fear of the LORD is the beginning of wisdom; a good understanding have all those who do His commandments. His praise endures forever.

Psalm 111:10

A good man deals graciously and lends; he will guide his affairs with discretion.

Psalm 112:5

The righteous man walks in his integrity; his children are blessed after him.

Proverbs 20:7

But if you have bitter envy and self-seeking in your hearts, do not boast and lie against the truth.

James 3:14

**Never rewrite your theology
to accommodate a desire.**

JESUS

And she will bring forth a Son, and you shall call His name JESUS, for He will save His people from their sins.

Matthew 1:21

For there is born to you this day in the city of David a Savior, who is Christ the Lord.

Luke 2:11

Then Jesus spoke to them again, saying, "I am the light of the world. He who follows Me shall not walk in darkness, but have the light of life."

John 8:12

I am the good shepherd. The good shepherd gives His life for the sheep.

John 10:11

Jesus said to her, "I am the resurrection and the life. He who believes in Me, though he may die, he shall live."

John 11:25

Jesus said to him, "I am the way, the truth, and the life. No one comes to the Father except through Me."

John 14:6

For there is one God and one Mediator between God and men, the Man Christ Jesus.

1 Timothy 2:5

His mind is keener than yours;
His memory is longer than yours;
His shoulders are bigger than yours.

JOY

You will show me the path of life; in Your presence is fullness of joy; at Your right hand are pleasures forevermore.

Psalm 16:11

And my soul shall be joyful in the LORD; it shall rejoice in His salvation.

Psalm 35:9

Blessed are the people who know the joyful sound! They walk, O LORD, in the light of Your countenance. In Your name they rejoice all day long, and in Your righteousness they are exalted.

Psalm 89:15,16

You have made known to me the ways of life; you will make me full of joy in Your presence.

Acts 2:28

For the kingdom of God is not eating and drinking, but righteousness and peace and joy in the Holy Spirit.

Romans 14:17

Happiness is when you like yourself.

LEADERSHIP

The steps of a good man are ordered by the LORD, and He delights in his way.

Psalm 37:23

For the LORD God is a sun and shield; the LORD will give grace and glory; no good thing will He withhold from those who walk uprightly.

Psalm 84:11

For with what judgment you judge, you will be judged; and with the measure you use, it will be measured back to you.

Matthew 7:2

For as many as are led by the Spirit of God, these are sons of God.

Romans 8:14

And the things that you have heard from me among many witnesses, commit these to faithful men who will be able to teach others also.

2 Timothy 2:2

Let the elders who rule well be counted worthy of double honor, especially those who labor in the word and doctrine. For the Scripture says, "You shall not muzzle an ox while it treads out the grain," and, "The laborer is worthy of his wages." Do not receive an accusation against an elder except from two or three witnesses. Those who are sinning rebuke in the presence of all, that the rest also may fear.

1 Timothy 5:17-20

The ability to follow is the first qualification for leadership.

LONELINESS

Behold, I am with you and will keep you wherever you go, and will bring you back to this land; for I will not leave you until I have done what I have spoken to you.

Genesis 28:15

And the LORD, He is the one who goes before you. He will be with you, He will not leave you nor forsake you; do not fear nor be dismayed.

Deuteronomy 31:8

Yea, though I walk through the valley of the shadow of death, I will fear no evil; for You are with me; Your rod and Your staff, they comfort me.

Psalm 23:4

When my father and my mother forsake me, then the LORD will take care of me.

Psalm 27:10

I will not leave you orphans; I will come to you.

John 14:18

For He Himself has said, "I will never leave you nor forsake you."

Hebrews 13:5b

Casting all your care upon Him, for He cares for you.

1 Peter 5:7

**Loneliness is not the absence of affection,
but the absence of direction.**

LOVE

Many waters cannot quench love, nor can the floods drown it. If a man would give for love all the wealth of his house, it would be utterly despised.

Song of Solomon 8:7

A new commandment I give to you, that you love one another; as I have loved you, that you also love one another. By this all will know that you are My disciples, if you have love for one another.

John 13:34,35

For the Father Himself loves you, because you have loved Me, and have believed that I came forth from God.

John 16:27

For this is the message that you heard from the beginning, that we should love one another.

1 John 3:11

Beloved, let us love one another, for love is of God; and everyone who loves is born of God and knows God. In this is love, not that we loved God, but that He loved us and sent His Son to be the propitiation for our sins.

1 John 4:7,10

What you respect you will attract, what you don't respect will move away from you.

LOYALTY

Be strong and of good courage, do not fear nor be afraid
of them; for the LORD your God, He is the One who goes
with you. He will not leave you nor forsake you.

Deuteronomy 31:6

A good man deals graciously and lends; he will guide his
affairs with discretion.

Psalm 112:5

Blessed are those who keep His testimonies, who seek
Him with the whole heart! You have commanded us to
keep Your precepts diligently.

Psalm 119.2,4

Discretion will preserve you; understanding will keep
you.

Proverbs 2.11

A man who has friends must himself be friendly, but
there is a friend who sticks closer than a brother.

Proverbs 18:24

Faithful are the wounds of a friend, but the kisses of an
enemy are deceitful.

Proverbs 27:6

Repay no one evil for evil. Have regard for good things in
the sight of all men.

Romans 12:17

**Give another what he cannot find anywhere
else and he will keep returning.**

LYING

I have hated those who regard useless idols; but I trust in the LORD.

Psalm 31:6

The truthful lip shall be established forever, but a lying tongue is but for a moment.

Proverbs 12:19

Blessed are you when they revile and persecute you, and say all kinds of evil against you falsely for My sake.

Matthew 5:11

Therefore, putting away lying, "Let each one of you speak truth with his neighbor," for we are members of one another.

Ephesians 4:25

For we know Him who said, "Vengeance is Mine, I will repay," says the Lord. And again, "The LORD will judge His people."

Hebrews 10:30

But the cowardly, unbelieving, abominable, murderers, sexually immoral, sorcerers, idolaters, and all liars shall have their part in the lake which burns with fire and brimstone, which is the second death.

Revelation 21:8

Those who will lie for you eventually will lie about you. Those who sin with you will eventually sin against you.

MENTORSHIP

And He Himself gave some to be apostles, some prophets, some evangelists, and some pastors and teachers, for the equipping of the saints for the work of ministry, for the edifying of the body of Christ.

Ephesians 4:11,12

Be diligent to present yourself approved to God, a worker who does not need to be ashamed, rightly dividing the word of truth.

2 Timothy 2:15

When I call to remembrance the genuine faith that is in you, which dwelt first in your grandmother Lois and your mother Eunice, and I am persuaded is in you also. Therefore I remind you to stir up the gift of God which is in you through the laying on of my hands.

2 Timothy 1:5,6

Now Joshua the son of Nun was full of the spirit of wisdom, for Moses had laid his hands on him; so the children of Israel heeded him, and did as the LORD had commanded Moses.

Deuteronomy 34:9

**Someone has heard what you have not;
someone has seen what you have not;
someone knows what you do not.
Your success depends on your
willingness to be mentored by them.**

MIRACLES

Ask, and it will be given to you; seek, and you will find; knock, and it will be opened to you.

Matthew 7:7

How God anointed Jesus of Nazareth with the Holy Spirit and with power, who went about doing good and healing all who were oppressed by the devil, for God was with Him.

Acts 10:38

For assuredly, I say to you, whoever says to this mountain, 'Be removed and be cast into the sea,' and does not doubt in his heart, but believes that those things he says will be done, he will have whatever he says. Therefore I say to you, whatever things you ask when you pray, believe that you receive them, and you will have them.

Mark 11:23,24

Ah, Lord God! Behold, You have made the heavens and the earth by Your great power and outstretched arm. There is nothing too hard for You.

Jeremiah 32:17

So Jesus stood still and commanded him to be brought to Him. And when he had come near, He asked him, saying, "What do you want Me to do for you?" He said, "Lord, that I may receive my sight." Then Jesus said to him, "Receive your sight; your faith has made you well." And immediately he received his sight, and followed Him, glorifying God. And all the people, when they saw it, gave praise to God.

Luke 18:40-43

**You're never as far from
a miracle as it first appears.**

MOTIVATION

Be strong and of good courage, do not fear nor be afraid of them; for the LORD your God, He is the One who goes with you. He will not leave you nor forsake you.

Deuteronomy 31:6

Have I not commanded you? Be strong and of good courage; do not be afraid, nor be dismayed, for the LORD your God is with you wherever you go.

Joshua 1:9

So he answered, "Do not fear, for those who are with us are more than those who are with them."

2 Kings 6:16

Through You we will push down our enemies; through Your name we will trample those who rise up against us.

Psalm 44:5

Therefore I will look to the LORD; I will wait for the God of my salvation; My God will hear me. When I fall, I will arise; When I sit in darkness, The LORD will be a light to me.

Micah 7:7,8b

I can do all things through Christ who strengthens me.

Philippians 4:13

**Discontentment is the catalyst for change.
Intolerance of the present creates a future.**

OBEDIENCE

Now therefore, if you will indeed obey My voice and keep My covenant, then you shall be a special treasure to Me above all people; for all the earth is Mine.

Exodus 19:5

But if you indeed obey His voice and do all that I speak, then I will be an enemy to your enemies and an adversary to your adversaries. For My Angel will go before you.

Exodus 23:22,23a

If you are willing and obedient, you shall eat the good of the land.

Isaiah 1:19

Whether it is pleasing or displeasing, we will obey the voice of the LORD our God.

Jeremiah 42:6a

Children, obey your parents in the Lord, for this is right.

Ephesians 6:1

For as by one man's disobedience many were made sinners, so also by one Man's obedience many will be made righteous.

Romans 5:19

Casting down arguments and every high thing that exalts itself against the knowledge of God, bringing every thought into captivity to the obedience of Christ.

2 Corinthians 10:5

**God will never advance you
beyond your last act of obedience.**

OPPOSITION

Rest in the LORD, and wait patiently for Him; do not fret because of him who prospers in his way, because of the man who brings wicked schemes to pass.

Psalm 37:7

In my distress I cried to the LORD, and He heard me. Deliver my soul, O LORD, from lying lips and from a deceitful tongue.

Psalm 120:1,2

"No weapon formed against you shall prosper, and every tongue which rises against you in judgment You shall condemn. This is the heritage of the servants of the LORD, and their righteousness is from Me," says the LORD.

Isaiah 54:17

When the enemy comes in like a flood, the Spirit of the LORD will lift up a standard against him.

Isaiah 59:19b

And who is he who will harm you if you become followers of what is good?

1 Peter 3:13

Casting all your care upon Him, for He cares for you.

1 Peter 5:7

Opposition is really the proof of progress.

Satan always attacks those next in line for a promotion.

OVERCOMING

Do not be overcome by evil, but overcome evil with good.

Romans 12:21

I write to you, young men, because you have overcome the wicked one. I write to you, little children, because you have known the Father.

1 John 2:13b

You are of God, little children, and have overcome them, because He who is in you is greater than he who is in the world.

1 John 4:4

To him who overcomes I will give to eat from the tree of life, which is in the midst of the Paradise of God.

Revelation 2:7b

To him who overcomes I will grant to sit with Me on My throne, as I also overcame and sat down with My Father on His throne.

Revelation 3:21

He who overcomes shall inherit all things, and I will be his God and he shall be My son.

Revelation 21:7

What you fail to master in your life will eventually master you.

PAIN

Look on my affliction and my pain, and forgive all my sins.

Psalm 25:18

Many are the afflictions of the righteous, but the LORD delivers him out of them all.

Psalm 34:19

Redeem me from the oppression of man.

Psalm 119:134a

He heals the brokenhearted and binds up their wounds.

Psalm 147:3

And one will say to him, 'What are these wounds between your arms?' Then he will answer, 'Those with which I was wounded in the house of my friends.'

Zechariah 13:6

And God will wipe away every tear from their eyes; there shall be no more death, nor sorrow, nor crying. There shall be no more pain, for the former things have passed away.

Revelation 21:4

**Pain is discomfort created by disorder.
It is not your enemy but merely
the proof that one exists.**

PATIENCE

Rest in the LORD, and wait patiently for Him; do not fret because of him who prospers in his way, because of the man who brings wicked schemes to pass.

Psalm 37:7

I waited patiently for the LORD; and He inclined to me, and heard my cry.

Psalm 40:1

And not only that, but we also glory in tribulations, knowing that tribulation produces perseverance; and perseverance, character; and character, hope. Now hope does not disappoint, because the love of God has been poured out in our hearts by the Holy Spirit who was given to us.

Romans 5:3-5

Rejoicing in hope, patient in tribulation, continuing steadfastly in prayer.

Romans 12:12

And let us not grow weary while doing good, for in due season we shall reap if we do not lose heart.

Galatians 6:9

Knowing that the testing of your faith produces patience. But let patience have its perfect work, that you may be perfect and complete, lacking nothing.

James 1:3,4

**Patience is the weapon that
forces deception to reveal itself.**

PEACE

I will both lie down in peace, and sleep; for You alone, O LORD, make me dwell in safety.

Psalm 4:8

Great peace have those who love Your law, and nothing causes them to stumble.

Psalm 119:165

You will keep him in perfect peace, whose mind is stayed on You, because he trusts in You. LORD, You will establish peace for us, for You have also done all our works in us.

Isaiah 26:3,12

Peace I leave with you, My peace I give to you; not as the world gives do I give to you. Let not your heart be troubled, neither let it be afraid.

John 14:27

For to be carnally minded is death, but to be spiritually minded is life and peace.

Romans 8:6

But the fruit of the Spirit is love, joy, peace, longsuffering, kindness, goodness, faithfulness.

Galatians 5:22

Now the fruit of righteousness is sown in peace by those who make peace.

James 3:18

**Peace is not the absence of conflict,
it's the absence of inner conflict.**

PEER PRESSURE

If your brother, the son of your mother, your son or your daughter, the wife of your bosom, or your friend who is as your own soul, secretly entices you, saying, 'Let us go and serve other gods,' which you have not known, neither you nor your fathers. You shall not consent to him or listen to him, nor shall your eye pity him, nor shall you spare him or conceal him.

Deuteronomy 13:6,8

My son, if sinners entice you, do not consent. If they say, "Come with us, let us lie in wait to shed blood; let us lurk secretly for the innocent without cause; let us swallow them alive like Sheol, and whole, like those who go down to the Pit; we shall find all kinds of precious possessions, we shall fill our houses with spoil; cast in your lot among us, let us all have one purse"; my son, do not walk in the way with them, keep your foot from their path.

Proverbs 1:10-15

For we do not have a High Priest who cannot sympathize with our weaknesses, but was in all points tempted as we are, yet without sin. Let us therefore come boldly to the throne of grace, that we may obtain mercy and find grace to help in time of need.

Hebrews 4:15,16

Satan's favorite entry point into your life is always through someone close to you.

PLANNING

In all your ways acknowledge Him, and He shall direct your paths.

Proverbs 3:6

Without counsel, plans go awry, but in the multitude of counselors they are established.

Proverbs 15:22

The preparations of the heart belong to man, but the answer of the tongue is from the LORD. A man's heart plans his way, but the LORD directs his steps.

Proverbs 16:1,9

There are many plans in a man's heart, nevertheless the Lord's counsel; that will stand.

Proverbs 19:21

The plans of the diligent lead surely to plenty, but those of everyone who is hasty, surely to poverty.

Proverbs 21:5

But a generous man devises generous things, and by generosity he shall stand.

Isaiah 32:8

For I know the thoughts that I think toward you, says the LORD, thoughts of peace and not of evil, to give you a future and a hope.

Jeremiah 29:11

**The season for research is
not the season for marketing.**

PRAYER

Seek the LORD and His strength; seek His face evermore!

1 Chronicles 16:11

If My people who are called by My name will humble themselves, and pray and seek My face, and turn from their wicked ways, then I will hear from heaven, and will forgive their sin and heal their land.

2 Chronicles 7:14

Watch and pray, lest you enter into temptation. The spirit indeed is willing, but the flesh is weak.

Matthew 26:41

Continue earnestly in prayer, being vigilant in it with thanksgiving.

Colossians 4:2

Pray without ceasing.

1 Thessalonians 5:17

The effective, fervent prayer of a righteous man avails much.

James 5:16b

But you, beloved, building yourselves up on your most holy faith, praying in the Holy Spirit.

Jude 20

One hour in the presence of God will reveal any flaw in your most carefully laid plans.

PROBLEM SOLVING

For we do not have a High Priest who cannot sympathize with our weaknesses, but was in all points tempted as we are, yet without sin. Let us therefore come boldly to the throne of grace, that we may obtain mercy and find grace to help in time of need.

Hebrews 4:15,16

He who heeds the word wisely will find good, and whoever trusts in the LORD, happy is he.

Proverbs 16:20

For which of you, intending to build a tower, does not sit down first and count the cost, whether he has enough to finish it.

Luke 14:28

Without counsel, plans go awry, but in the multitude of counselors they are established.

Proverbs 15:22

And if we know that He hears us, whatever we ask, we know that we have the petitions that we have asked of Him

1 John 5:15

You will only be remembered in life by the problems you solve and the ones you create. You will only be pursued for the problems you solve. The problem that infuriates you the most is the problem God has assigned you to solve.

PRODUCTIVITY

Unless the LORD builds the house, they labor in vain who build it; unless the LORD guards the city, the watchman stays awake in vain.

Psalm 127:1

A wise man will hear and increase learning, and a man of understanding will attain wise counsel.

Proverbs 1:5

But other seed fell on good ground and yielded a crop that sprang up, increased and produced: some thirtyfold, some sixty, and some a hundred.

Mark 4:8

Most assuredly, I say to you, unless a grain of wheat falls into the ground and dies, it remains alone; but if it dies, it produces much grain.

John 12:24

I am the vine, you are the branches. He who abides in Me, and I in him, bears much fruit; for without Me you can do nothing. By this My Father is glorified, that you bear much fruit; so you will be My disciples.

John 15:5,8

That you may walk worthy of the Lord, fully pleasing Him, being fruitful in every good work and increasing in the knowledge of God.

Colossians 1:10

The quality of your preparation determines the quality of your performance.

PROMOTION

For exaltation comes neither from the east nor from the west nor from the south. But God is the Judge: He puts down one, and exalts another.

Psalm 75:6,7

The wise shall inherit glory, but shame shall be the legacy of fools.

Proverbs 3:35

Wisdom is the principal thing; therefore get wisdom. And in all your getting, get understanding. Exalt her, and she will promote you; she will bring you honor, when you embrace her. She will place on your head an ornament of grace; a crown of glory she will deliver to you.

Proverbs 4:7-9

O LORD, I know the way of man is not in himself; it is not in man who walks to direct his own steps.

Jeremiah 10:23

I press toward the goal for the prize of the upward call of God in Christ Jesus.

Philippians 3:14

**Someone is always observing you who
is capable of greatly blessing you.
You will never be promoted until you become
overqualified for your present position.**

PROSPERITY

Blessed is the man who walks not in the counsel of the ungodly, nor stands in the path of sinners, nor sits in the seat of the scornful; but his delight is in the law of the LORD, and in His law he meditates day and night. He shall be like a tree planted by the rivers of water, that brings forth its fruit in its season, whose leaf also shall not wither; and whatever he does shall prosper.

Psalm 1:1-3

If they obey and serve Him, they shall spend their days in prosperity, and their years in pleasures.

Job 36:11

Let the LORD be magnified, Who has pleasure in the prosperity of His servant.

Psalm 35:27b

Beloved, I pray that you may prosper in all things and be in health, just as your soul prospers.

3 John 2

You shall diligently keep the commandments of the LORD your God, His testimonies, and His statutes which He has commanded you. That you may go in and possess the good land of which the LORD swore to your fathers.

Deuteronomy 6:17,18b

Prosperity is having enough of God's provision to complete His instructions for your life.

PROTECTION

Yea, though I walk through the valley of the shadow of death, I will fear no evil; for You are with me; Your rod and Your staff, they comfort me. You prepare a table before me in the presence of my enemies; You anoint my head with oil; my cup runs over.

Psalm 23:4,5

He who dwells in the secret place of the Most High Shall abide under the shadow of the Almighty. He shall cover you with His feathers, and under His wings you shall take refuge; His truth shall be your shield and buckler. You shall not be afraid of the terror by night, nor of the arrow that flies by day, nor of the pestilence that walks in darkness, nor of the destruction that lays waste at noonday. A thousand may fall at your side, and ten thousand at your right hand; but it shall not come near you. No evil shall befall you, nor shall any plague come near your dwelling, for He shall give His angels charge over you, to keep you in all your ways.

Psalm 91:1,4-7,10,11

"And I will rebuke the devourer for your sakes, so that he will not destroy the fruit of your ground, nor shall the vine fail to bear fruit for you in the field," Says the LORD of hosts.

Malachi 3:11

Protection is produced through partnership.

91

RACISM

A new commandment I give to you, that you love one another; as I have loved you, that you also love one another.

John 13:34

There is neither Jew nor Greek, there is neither slave nor free, there is neither male nor female; for you are all one in Christ Jesus.

Galatians 3:28

And walk in love, as Christ also has loved us and given Himself for us, an offering and a sacrifice to God for a sweet-smelling aroma.

Ephesians 5:2

But he who does wrong will be repaid for what he has done, and there is no partiality.

Colossians 3:25

If you really fulfill the royal law according to the Scripture, "You shall love your neighbor as yourself," you do well; but if you show partiality, you commit sin, and are convicted by the law as transgressors.

James 2:8,9

Your significance is not in your similarity to another but in your point of difference from another.

REJECTION

Behold what manner of love the Father has bestowed on us, that we should be called children of God! Therefore the world does not know us, because it did not know Him.

1 John 3:1

And let us not grow weary while doing good, for in due season we shall reap if we do not lose heart.

Galatians 6:9

A man who has friends must himself be friendly, but there is a friend who sticks closer than a brother.

Proverbs 18:24

For the LORD will not cast off His people, nor will He forsake His inheritance.

Psalm 94:14

All that the Father gives Me will come to Me, and the one who comes to Me I will by no means cast out. For I have come down from heaven, not to do My own will, but the will of Him who sent Me. This is the will of the Father who sent Me, that of all He has given Me I should lose nothing, but should raise it up at the last day.

John 6:37-39

**Those who created yesterday's pain
do not control tomorrow's potential.**

REPENTANCE

If we confess our sins, He is faithful and just to forgive us our sins and to cleanse us from all unrighteousness.

1 John 1:9

You have forgiven the iniquity of Your people; You have covered all their sin. Selah

Psalm 85:2

Let the wicked forsake his way, and the unrighteous man his thoughts; let him return to the LORD, and He will have mercy on him; and to our God, for He will abundantly pardon.

Isaiah 55:7

For I will be merciful to their unrighteousness, and their sins and their lawless deeds I will remember no more.

Hebrews 8:12

And whenever you stand praying, if you have anything against anyone, forgive him, that your Father in heaven may also forgive you your trespasses.

Mark 11:25

All men fall. The great ones get back up.

REPUTATION

Blessed is the man who walks not in the counsel of the ungodly, nor stands in the path of sinners, nor sits in the seat of the scornful; but his delight is in the law of the LORD, and in His law he meditates day and night.

Psalm 1:1,2

All the paths of the LORD are mercy and truth, to such as keep His covenant and His testimonies. Let integrity and uprightness preserve me, for I wait for You.

Psalm 25:10,21

But as for me, I will walk in my integrity; redeem me and be merciful to me.

Psalm 26:11

But made Himself of no reputation, taking the form of a bondservant, and coming in the likeness of men. And being found in appearance as a man, He humbled Himself and became obedient to the point of death, even the death of the cross.

Philippians 2:7,8

He who heeds the word wisely will find good, and whoever trusts in the LORD, happy is he.

Proverbs 16:20

**You will be remembered for the pain
or the pleasure you have created.**

RESPONSIBILITY

Let us hear the conclusion of the whole matter: fear God and keep His commandments, for this is man's all.

Ecclesiastes 12:13

You are the salt of the earth; but if the salt loses its flavor, how shall it be seasoned? It is then good for nothing but to be thrown out and trampled underfoot by men. You are the light of the world. A city that is set on a hill cannot be hidden. Nor do they light a lamp and put it under a basket, but on a lampstand, and it gives light to all who are in the house. Let your light so shine before men, that they may see your good works and glorify your Father in heaven. Whoever therefore breaks one of the least of these commandments, and teaches men so, shall be called least in the kingdom of heaven; but whoever does and teaches them, he shall be called great in the kingdom of heaven.

Matthew 5:13-16,19

Then Jesus said to His disciples, "If anyone desires to come after Me, let him deny himself, and take up his cross, and follow Me. For whoever desires to save his life will lose it, but whoever loses his life for My sake will find it."

Matthew 16:24,25

**When you do what you can,
God will do what you can't.**

REST

And on the seventh day God ended His work which He had done, and He rested on the seventh day from all His work which He had done.

Genesis 2:2

Therefore my heart is glad, and my glory rejoices; my flesh also will rest in hope.

Psalm 16:9

For with stammering lips and another tongue He will speak to this people, to whom He said, "This is the rest with which You may cause the weary to rest," and, "This is the refreshing"; yet they would not hear.

Isaiah 28:11,12

Come to Me, all you who labor and are heavy laden, and I will give you rest.

Matthew 11:28

To everything there is a season, a time for every purpose under heaven. A time to love, and a time to hate; a time of war, and a time of peace.

Ecclesiastes 3:1,8

Take My yoke upon you and learn from Me, for I am gentle and lowly in heart, and you will find rest for your souls. For My yoke is easy and My burden is light.

Matthew 11:29,30

**When fatigue walks in faith walks out.
Tired eyes rarely see a good future.**

RICHES

Praise the LORD! Blessed is the man who fears the LORD, who delights greatly in His commandments. His descendants will be mighty on earth; the generation of the upright will be blessed. Wealth and riches will be in his house, and his righteousness endures forever.

Psalm 112:1-3

Happy is the man who finds wisdom, and the man who gains understanding; length of days is in her (wisdom's) right hand, in her left hand riches and honor.

Proverbs 3:13,16

The wealth of the sinner is stored up for the righteous.

Proverbs 13:22b

Do not lay up for yourselves treasures on earth, where moth and rust destroy and where thieves break in and steal; but lay up for yourselves treasures in heaven, where neither moth nor rust destroys and where thieves do not break in and steal.

Matthew 6:19,20

And you shall remember the LORD your God, for it is He who gives you power to get wealth, that He may establish His covenant which He swore to your fathers, as it is this day.

Deuteronomy 8:18

Some study the exit of every penny, others study the entry of every dollar. The wise do both.

RIGHTEOUSNESS

For He made Him who knew no sin to be sin for us, that
we might become the righteousness of God in Him.

2 Corinthians 5:21

And be found in Him, not having my own righteousness,
which is from the law, but that which is through faith in
Christ, the righteousness which is from God by faith.

Philippians 3:9

Even the righteousness of God, through faith in Jesus
Christ, to all and on all who believe. For there is no difference.

Romans 3:22

But to him who does not work but believes on Him who
justifies the ungodly, his faith is accounted for righteousness.

Romans 4:5

The work of righteousness will be peace, and the effect
of righteousness, quietness and assurance forever.

Isaiah 32:17

**Your integrity will always be remembered
longer than your product.**

SALVATION

All we like sheep have gone astray; we have turned, every one, to his own way; and the LORD has laid on Him the iniquity of us all.

Isaiah 53:6

But as many as received Him, to them He gave the right to become children of God, to those who believe in His name.

John 1:12

The one who comes to Me I will by no means cast out.
John 6:37b

So they said, "Believe on the Lord Jesus Christ, and you will be saved, you and your household."

Acts 16:31

For all have sinned and fall short of the glory of God.
Romans 3:23

That if you confess with your mouth the Lord Jesus and believe in your heart that God has raised Him from the dead, you will be saved. For with the heart one believes unto righteousness, and with the mouth confession is made unto salvation.

Romans 10:9,10

**God never consults your past
to determine your future.**

SCHEDULE

Commit your way to the LORD, trust also in Him, and He shall bring it to pass.

Psalm 37:5

And let the beauty of the LORD our God be upon us, and establish the work of our hands for us; yes, establish the work of our hands.

Psalm 90:17

And let us not grow weary while doing good, for in due season we shall reap if we do not lose heart.

Galatians 6:9

Redeeming the time, because the days are evil.

Ephesians 5:16

Your ears shall hear a word behind you, saying, "This is the way, walk in it," whenever you turn to the right hand or whenever you turn to the left.

Isaiah 30:21

For the vision is yet for an appointed time; but at the end it will speak, and it will not lie. Though it tarries, wait for it; because it will surely come, it will not tarry.

Habakkuk 2:3

Those who do not respect your time will not respect your wisdom either.

SELF-CONFIDENCE

The LORD is my light and my salvation; whom shall I fear? The LORD is the strength of my life; of whom shall I be afraid?

Psalm 27:1

It is better to trust in the LORD than to put confidence in man.

Psalm 118:8

For the LORD will be your confidence, and will keep your foot from being caught.

Proverbs 3:26

See, I have inscribed you on the palms of My hands; your walls are continually before Me.

Isaiah 49:16

You did not choose Me, but I chose you and appointed you that you should go and bear fruit, and that your fruit should remain.

John 15:16a

Being confident of this very thing, that He who has begun a good work in you will complete it until the day of Jesus Christ.

Philippians 1:6

You are of God, little children, and have overcome them, because He who is in you is greater than he who is in the world.

1 John 4:4

I can do all things through Christ who strengthens me.

Philippians 4:13

**You were created for accomplishment.
You are engineered for success.**

SEX

He who covers his sins will not prosper, but whoever confesses and forsakes them will have mercy.

Proverbs 28:13

Flee sexual immorality. Every sin that a man does is outside the body, but he who commits sexual immorality sins against his own body.

1 Corinthians 6:18

Or do you not know that your body is the temple of the Holy Spirit who is in you, whom you have from God, and you are not your own? Therefore glorify God in your body and in your spirit, which are God's.

1 Corinthians 6:19,20b

Nevertheless, because of sexual immorality, let each man have his own wife, and let each woman have her own husband.

1 Corinthians 7:2

No temptation has overtaken you except such as is common to man, but God is faithful, who will not allow you to be tempted beyond what you are able, but with the temptation will also make the way of escape, that you may be able to bear it.

1 Corinthians 10:13

**Power is the ability to walk away
from something you desire
to protect something you love.**

SIN

Do not remember the sins of my youth, nor my transgressions; according to Your mercy remember me, for Your goodness' sake, O LORD.

Psalm 25:7

Hide Your face from my sins, and blot out all my iniquities.

Psalm 51:9

If I regard iniquity in my heart, the LORD will not hear.

Psalm 66:18

With my whole heart I have sought You; oh, let me not wander from Your commandments! Your word I have hidden in my heart, that I might not sin against You!

Psalm 119:10,11

He who covers his sins will not prosper, but whoever confesses and forsakes them will have mercy.

Proverbs 28:13

For all have sinned and fall short of the glory of God.

Romans 3:23

If we confess our sins, He is faithful and just to forgive us our sins and to cleanse us from all unrighteousness.

1 John 1:9

What you fail to destroy in your life will eventually destroy you.

SOUL WINNING

The fruit of the righteous is a tree of life, and he who wins souls is wise.

Proverbs 11:30

Then He said to His disciples, "The harvest truly is plentiful, but the laborers are few."

Matthew 9:37

He who is not with Me is against Me, and he who does not gather with Me scatters abroad.

Matthew 12:30

And He said to them, "Go into all the world and preach the gospel to every creature. He who believes and is baptized will be saved; but he who does not believe will be condemned."

Mark 16:15,16

Jesus answered and said to him, "Most assuredly, I say to you, unless one is born again, he cannot see the kingdom of God."

John 3:3

Do you not say, "There are still four months and then comes the harvest"? Behold, I say to you, lift up your eyes and look at the fields, for they are already white for harvest!

John 4:35

The broken become masters at mending.

STRESS

The LORD also will be a refuge for the oppressed, a refuge in times of trouble.

Psalm 9:9

My flesh and my heart fail; but God is the strength of my heart and my portion forever.

Psalm 73:26

A thousand may fall at your side, and ten thousand at your right hand; but it shall not come near you. No evil shall befall you, nor shall any plague come near your dwelling.

Psalm 91:7,10

It is vain for you to rise up early, to sit up late, to eat the bread of sorrows; for so He gives His beloved sleep.

Psalm 127:2

Casting all your care upon Him, for He cares for you.

1 Peter 5:7

Peace I leave with you, My peace I give to you; not as the world gives do I give to you. Let not your heart be troubled, neither let it be afraid.

John 14:27

Whenever I am afraid, I will trust in You.

Psalm 56:3

Never complain about what you permit.

SUCCESS

But he said to me, "The LORD, before whom I walk, will send His angel with you and prosper your way."

Genesis 24:40a

Therefore keep the words of this covenant, and do them, that you may prosper in all that you do.

Deuteronomy 29:9

Only be strong and very courageous, that you may observe to do according to all the law which Moses My servant commanded you; do not turn from it to the right hand or to the left, that you may prosper wherever you go. This Book of the Law shall not depart from your mouth, but you shall meditate in it day and night, that you may observe to do according to all that is written in it. For then you will make your way prosperous, and then you will have good success.

Joshua 1:7,8

Pray for the peace of Jerusalem: "May they prosper who love you."

Psalm 122:6

Honor the LORD with your possessions, and with the first-fruits of all your increase; so your barns will be filled with plenty, and your vats will overflow with new wine.

Proverbs 3:9,10

**Your success is determined by
the problems you solve for others.**

SUICIDAL THOUGHTS

You shall not murder.

Exodus 20:13

The LORD is my light and my salvation; whom shall I fear? The LORD is the strength of my life; of whom shall I be afraid? Though an army may encamp against me, my heart shall not fear; though war should rise against me, in this I will be confident. For in the time of trouble He shall hide me in His pavilion; in the secret place of His tabernacle He shall hide me; He shall set me high upon a rock.

Psalm 27:1,3,5

Your word I have hidden in my heart, that I might not sin against You!

Psalm 119:11

I will praise You, for I am fearfully and wonderfully made; marvelous are Your works, and that my soul knows very well.

Psalm 139:14

Being confident of this very thing, that He who has begun a good work in you will complete it until the day of Jesus Christ.

Philippians 1:6

Weeping may endure for a night, but joy comes in the morning.

Psalm 30:5b

**Your focus determines what you feel.
When you change your focus
you change your feelings.**

TEAMWORK

Behold, how good and how pleasant it is for brethren to dwell together in unity!

Psalm 133:1

Two are better than one, because they have a good reward for their labor. For if they fall, one will lift up his companion. But woe to him who is alone when he falls, for he has no one to help him up. Though one may be overpowered by another, two can withstand him. And a threefold cord is not quickly broken.

Ecclesiastes 4:9,10,12

Can two walk together, unless they are agreed?

Amos 3:3

Again I say to you that if two of you agree on earth concerning anything that they ask, it will be done for them by My Father in heaven.

Matthew 18:19

When the Day of Pentecost had fully come, they were all with one accord in one place.

Acts 2:1

Knowing that whatever good anyone does, he will receive the same from the Lord, whether he is a slave or free.

Ephesians 6:8

**What you make happen for others,
God will make happen for you.**

109

TEMPTATION

Your word I have hidden in my heart, that I might not sin against You!

Psalm 119:11

No temptation has overtaken you except such as is common to man; but God is faithful, who will not allow you to be tempted beyond what you are able, but with the temptation will also make the way of escape, that you may be able to bear it.

1 Corinthians 10:13

Put on the whole armor of God, that you may be able to stand against the wiles of the devil. Above all, taking the shield of faith with which you will be able to quench all the fiery darts of the wicked one.

Ephesians 6:11,16

Therefore submit to God. Resist the devil and he will flee from you.

James 4:7

Then the Lord knows how to deliver the godly out of temptations.

2 Peter 2:9a

When the enemy comes in like a flood, the Spirit of the LORD will lift up a standard against him.

Isaiah 59:19b

What you're willing to walk away from determines what God will bring to you.

TEN COMMANDMENTS

You shall have no other gods before Me.

You shall not make for yourself a carved image.

You shall not take the name of the LORD your God in vain.

Remember the Sabbath day, to keep it holy.

Honor your father and your mother.

You shall not murder.

You shall not commit adultery.

You shall not steal.

You shall not bear false witness against your neighbor.

You shall not covet anything that is your neighbor's.

Taken from Exodus 20:3-17

**Your future is determined
by your ability to follow instructions.**

THOUGHTS

Many, O LORD my God, are Your wonderful works which You have done; and Your thoughts toward us cannot be recounted to You in order; if I would declare and speak of them, they are more than can be numbered.

Psalm 40:5

The thoughts of the righteous are right, but the counsels of the wicked are deceitful.

Proverbs 12:5

Commit your works to the LORD, and your thoughts will be established.

Proverbs 16:3

For as he thinks in his heart, so is he.

Proverbs 23:7a

For I know the thoughts that I think toward you, says the LORD, thoughts of peace and not of evil, to give you a future and a hope.

Jeremiah 29:11

Finally, brethren, whatever things are true, whatever things are noble, whatever things are just, whatever things are pure, whatever things are lovely, whatever things are of good report, if there is any virtue and if there is anything praiseworthy; meditate on these things.

Philippians 4:8

**Losers focus on what they are
going through while champions focus
on what they are going to.**

TITHING

You shall truly tithe all the increase of your grain that the field produces year by year.

Deuteronomy 14:22

Honor the LORD with your possessions, and with the first-fruits of all your increase; so your barns will be filled with plenty, and your vats will overflow with new wine.

Proverbs 3:9,10

"Bring all the tithes into the storehouse, that there may be food in My house, and try Me now in this," Says the LORD of hosts, "If I will not open for you the windows of heaven and pour out for you such blessing that there will not be room enough to receive it. And I will rebuke the devourer for your sakes, So that he will not destroy the fruit of your ground, nor shall the vine fail to bear fruit for you in the field," says the LORD of hosts.

Malachi 3:10,11

Woe to you, scribes and Pharisees, hypocrites! For you pay tithe of mint and anise and cummin, and have neglected the weightier matters of the law: justice and mercy and faith. These you ought to have done, without leaving the others undone.

Matthew 23:23

**When you let go of what is in your hand
God will let go of what's in his hand.
Tithe is a measure of your obedience,
an offering is a measure of your generosity.**

TRUTH

All the paths of the LORD are mercy and truth, to such as keep His covenant and His testimonies.

Psalm 25:10

Jesus said to him, "I am the way, the truth, and the life. No one comes to the Father except through Me."

John 14:6

Finally, brethren, whatever things are true, whatever things are noble, whatever things are just, whatever things are pure, whatever things are lovely, whatever things are of good report, if there is any virtue and if there is anything praiseworthy; meditate on these things.

Philippians 4:8

Since you have purified your souls in obeying the truth through the Spirit in sincere love of the brethren, love one another fervently with a pure heart.

1 Peter 1:22

God is not a man, that He should lie, nor a son of man, that He should repent. Has He said, and will He not do? Or has He spoken, and will He not make it good?

Numbers 23:19

**Truth is the most powerful thing
on earth because it is the only thing
that cannot be changed.**

UNEMPLOYMENT

Trust in the LORD, and do good; dwell in the land, and feed on His faithfulness.

Psalm 37:3

Behold, I will do a new thing, now it shall spring forth; shall you not know it? I will even make a road in the wilderness and rivers in the desert.

Isaiah 43:19

Do not love sleep, lest you come to poverty; open your eyes, and you will be satisfied with bread.

Proverbs 20:13

Whatever your hand finds to do, do it with your might.

Ecclesiastes 9:10a

For assuredly, I say to you, whoever says to this mountain, 'Be removed and be cast into the sea,' and does not doubt in his heart, but believes that those things he says will be done, he will have whatever he says.

Mark 11:23

**Go where you're celebrated,
not where you're tolerated.**

VICTORY

Then Moses and the children of Israel sang this song to the LORD, and spoke, saying: "I will sing to the LORD, for He has triumphed gloriously! The horse and its rider He has thrown into the sea!"

Exodus 15:1

O my God, I trust in You; let me not be ashamed; let not my enemies triumph over me.

Psalm 25:2

For You, LORD, have made me glad through Your work; I will triumph in the works of Your hands.

Psalm 92:4

Save us, O LORD our God, and gather us from among the Gentiles, to give thanks to Your holy name, to triumph in Your praise.

Psalm 106:47

And they overcame him by the blood of the Lamb and by the word of their testimony, and they did not love their lives to the death.

Revelation 12:11

I can do all things through Christ who strengthens me.

Philippians 4:13

Champions simply make an extra attempt.

VISION

In a dream, in a vision of the night, when deep sleep falls upon men, while slumbering on their beds, then He opens the ears of men, and seals their instruction. In order to turn man from his deed, and conceal pride from man.

Job 33:15-17

Where there is no revelation, the people cast off restraint; but happy is he who keeps the law.

Proverbs 29:18

"Write the vision and make it plain on tablets, that he may run who reads it." For the vision is yet for an appointed time; but at the end it will speak, and it will not lie. Though it tarries, wait for it; because it will surely come, it will not tarry.

Habakkuk 2:2a,3

Enlarge the place of your tent, and let them stretch out the curtains of your dwellings; do not spare, lengthen your cords, and strengthen your stakes.

Isaiah 54:2

And it shall come to pass afterward that I will pour out My Spirit on all flesh; your sons and your daughters shall prophesy, your old men shall dream dreams, your young men shall see visions.

Joel 2:28

**Stop looking at where you have been
and start looking at where you can be.**

117

VOWS

When you make a vow to the LORD your God, you shall not delay to pay it; for the LORD your God will surely require it of you, and it would be sin to you.

Deuteronomy 23:21

If a man makes a vow to the LORD, or swears an oath to bind himself by some agreement, he shall not break his word; he shall do according to all that proceeds out of his mouth.

Numbers 30:2

Make vows to the LORD your God, and pay them; let all who are around Him bring presents to Him who ought to be feared.

Psalm 76:11

He who has pity on the poor lends to the LORD, and He will pay back what he has given.

Proverbs 19:17

Better not to vow than to vow and not pay.

Ecclesiastes 5:5

The waves of yesterday's broken vows will splash on the shores of tomorrow.

WEALTH

And you shall remember the LORD your God, for it is He who gives you power to get wealth, that He may establish His covenant which He swore to your fathers, as it is this day.

Deuteronomy 8:18

Praise the LORD! Blessed is the man who fears the LORD, who delights greatly in His commandments. His descendants will be mighty on earth; the generation of the upright will be blessed. Wealth and riches will be in his house, and his righteousness endures forever.

Psalm 112:1-3

The wealth of the sinner is stored up for the righteous.

Proverbs 13:22b

Command those who are rich in this present age not to be haughty, nor to trust in uncertain riches but in the living God, who gives us richly all things to enjoy. Let them do good, that they be rich in good works, ready to give, willing to share, storing up for themselves a good foundation for the time to come, that they may lay hold on eternal life.

1 Timothy 6:17-19

And He said to them, "Take heed and beware of covetousness, for one's life does not consist in the abundance of the things he possesses."

Luke 12:15

**Wealth is when you have
a lot of something you love.**

WINNING

Then Moses and the children of Israel sang this song to the LORD, and spoke, saying: "I will sing to the LORD, for He has triumphed gloriously! The horse and its rider He has thrown into the sea!"

Exodus 15:1

For You, LORD, have made me glad through Your work; I will triumph in the works of Your hands.

Psalm 92:4

The fruit of the righteous is a tree of life, and he who wins souls is wise.

Proverbs 11:30

For I will give you a mouth and wisdom which all your adversaries will not be able to contradict or resist.

Luke 21:15

You are of God, little children, and have overcome them, because He who is in you is greater than he who is in the world.

1 John 4:4

Those who do wickedly against the covenant he shall corrupt with flattery; but the people who know their God shall be strong, and carry out great exploits.

Daniel 11:32

So he answered and said to me: "This is the word of the LORD to Zerubbabel: 'Not by might nor by power, but by My Spirit,' says the LORD of hosts.

Zechariah 4:6

**The first step toward success
is the willingness to listen.**

WISDOM

Wisdom and knowledge are granted to you; and I will give you riches and wealth and honor, such as none of the kings have had who were before you, nor shall any after you have the like.

2 Chronicles 1:12

The fear of the LORD is the beginning of wisdom; a good understanding have all those who do His commandments. His praise endures forever.

Psalm 111:10

Wisdom is the principal thing; therefore get wisdom. And in all your getting, get understanding. Exalt her, and she will promote you; she will bring you honor, when you embrace her.

Proverbs 4:7,8

If any of you lacks wisdom, let him ask of God, who gives to all liberally and without reproach, and it will be given to him.

James 1:5

Happy is the man who finds wisdom, and the man who gains understanding

Proverbs 3:13

**Wisdom is the only real
need you will ever have.**

WORK

Work shall be done for six days, but the seventh day shall be a holy day for you, a Sabbath of rest to the LORD.

Exodus 35:2a

The LORD your God may bless you in all the work of your hands.

Deuteronomy 24:19b

'Be strong, all you people of the land,' says the LORD, 'and work; for I am with you,' says the LORD of hosts.

Haggai 2:4b

The people had a mind to work.

Nehemiah 4:6b

A worker is worthy of his food.

Matthew 10:10b

Six days you shall labor and do all your work.

Exodus 20:9

Moreover it is required in stewards that one be found faithful.

1 Corinthians 4:2

Do you see a man who excels in his work? He will stand before kings; he will not stand before unknown men.

Proverbs 22:29

**Money is merely a reward
for solving problems.**

WORRY

And you would be secure, because there is hope; yes, you would dig around you, and take your rest in safety.

Job 11:18

Do not fret because of evildoers, nor be envious of the wicked.

Proverbs 24:19

In righteousness you shall be established; you shall be far from oppression, for you shall not fear; and from terror, for it shall not come near you.

Isaiah 54:14

Be anxious for nothing, but in everything by prayer and supplication, with thanksgiving, let your requests be made known to God; and the peace of God, which surpasses all understanding, will guard your hearts and minds through Christ Jesus. Finally, brethren, whatever things are true, whatever things are noble, whatever things are just, whatever things are pure, whatever things are lovely, whatever things are of good report, if there is any virtue and if there is anything praiseworthy, meditate on these things.

Philipplans 4:6-8

Do not fear therefore; you are of more value than many sparrows.

Matthew 10:31

Nothing is ever as bad as it first appears.

WORSHIP

Give to the LORD the glory due His name; bring an offering, and come before Him. Oh, worship the LORD in the beauty of holiness!

1 Chronicles 16:29

It is good to give thanks to the LORD, and to sing praises to Your name, O Most High; to declare Your lovingkindness in the morning, and Your faithfulness every night.

Psalm 92:1,2

Now we know that God does not hear sinners; but if anyone is a worshiper of God and does His will, He hears him.

John 9:31

I will extol You, my God, O King; and I will bless Your name forever and ever. Every day I will bless You, and I will praise Your name forever and ever. Great is the LORD, and greatly to be praised; and His greatness is unsearchable.

Psalm 145:1-3

And Jesus answered and said to him, "Get behind Me, Satan! For it is written, 'You shall worship the LORD your God, and Him only you shall serve.'"

Luke 4:8

**True worship is not forced past.
It's an unavoidable intimacy. It's the
love-room where your future is born.**

What Is Your Decision?

If you have never received Jesus Christ as your personal Lord and Savior, why not do it right now? Simply repeat this prayer with sincerity: "Lord Jesus, I believe that You are the Son of God. I believe that You became man and died on the cross for my sins. I believe that God raised You from the dead and made You the Savior of the world. I confess that I am a sinner and I ask You to forgive me, and to cleanse me of all my sins. I accept Your forgiveness, and I receive You as my Lord and Savior. In Jesus' name, I pray. Amen."

"...if you confess with your mouth, 'Jesus is Lord,' and believe in your heart that God raised him from the dead, you will be saved. For it is with your heart that you believe and are justified, and it is with your mouth that you confess and are saved....for, 'Everyone who calls on the name of the Lord will be saved.'"

Romans 10:9,10,13 NIV

"If we confess our sins, he is faithful and just and will forgive us our sins and purify us from all unrighteousness."

1 John 1:9 NIV

Now that you have accepted Jesus as your Savior:

1. Read your Bible *daily* – it is your spiritual food that will make you a strong Christian.

2. Pray and talk to God *daily* – He desires for the two of you to communicate and share your lives with each other.

3. Share your faith with others – be bold to let others know that Jesus loves them.

4. Regularly attend a local church where Jesus is preached, where you can serve Him and where you can fellowship with other believers.

5. Let His love in your heart touch the lives of others by your good works done in His name.

Please let us know of the decision you made.

Write:

Honor Books
P.O. Box 55388
Tulsa, OK 74155

Other copies in the *One-Minute Pocket Bible*
series include:

One-Minute Pocket Bible for Teenagers
One-Minute Pocket Bible for Women
One-Minute Pocket Bible for Men

Available at your local bookstore.

Tulsa, Oklahoma 74155